7 Minute Secrets to a Successful Life & Career

Duane Alley

DUANE ALLEY

7 Secrets to a Successful Life and Career

Copyright © 2011 by Duane Alley – http://www.duanealley.com

All rights reserved. No part of this book may be produced or utilised in any form or by any means, electronic or mechanical, including photocopying, recording or by any information storage and retrieval system, without permission in writing from the Publisher.

Published 2011

Publisher: Performance Results Pty Ltd

Graphic Design & Layout: Mélissa Caron – Enki Communications – Go-Enki.com
Editor: Richard Burian – Enki Communications – Go-Enki.com

Self Help

ISBN 978-0-9870571-1-2

For my Nephew & best Pal, Michael Alley.

You are my greatest reason to get up

better & be thank-full every day.

Table of Contents

About the Author 13

Introduction: Foreword 15

Day 0 - Bonus 7 Minute Secrets 19

Day 1 - The Secret of Rewarding Yourself 25

Day 2 - Your second 7 Minute Secret 31

Day 3 - The Secret of Asking for Green Lights 37

Day 4 - The Secret of Gratitude 43

Day 5 - The Secret of Gratitude to Others 49

Day 6 - The Secret of Doing 55

Day 7 - Your Last 7 Minute Secret... Sort Of 63

Afterthoughts 69

6-Week Workbook 73

Testimonials
What they are saying about us...

> Hey Duane - just wanted to let you know I have been using your 7 Minute Secrets in daily life - especially the stretch, smile, grateful outside, grateful inside and it has totally changed my day for the better! More energy, more positivity = getting more done, happier co-workers and happier me at the end of the day! As a coach its important for me to help my clients make money as well as get happy. This seemingly simple thing has had great positive effects on them as well as myself. Thank you!
>
> **Elisa Zegna**

> Hi Duane,
> I've come to realize that more often than not, that the small things in life are the things that make the most difference in our lives. Your "7 Minute Secrets" is the one small thing that I can do everyday that makes the biggest difference for me. The simple act of smiling, stretching (just a little), drinking some water, looking for beauty both inside and out and saying "Thank you" out loud is all it takes to make a huge and positive difference every minute of everyday.
>
> So thank you Duane. I am a grateful recipient of your mission. I look forward to staying in touch, to growing, learning and expanding with you.
>
> **Connie Dorigan, CPC - Dorigan & Associates**
> *"I find hidden tech talent for companies"*
> *www.dorigan.com*

> Duane has captured the essence of what produces results and fulfilment in life. His 7 Minute Secrets are simple yet effective showing you how to apply the attitude of gratitude to your life. These secrets of appreciation and doing the little things are core to your success. Enjoy!
>
> **Annette Huygens-Tholen – Author of Success beyond Sport; Olympian, International Speaker, Success Coach**

> Hi Duane,
>
> I have realized during the program and specially after doing it on my own, that the easiest thing is to change myself and not wait for the circumstances to change.
>
> It is a Saturday morning now and it is raining cats and dogs and do I still smile and look forward to my day ahead of me? You bet I do.
>
> Planning my week ahead helped me to accomplish those things as well that I was postponing. My gratitude feelings towards life have increased and I am much more fun to be with. I also found my motto for life: Enjoy creating new changes i.e oppotunities in your life. – I do.
>
> Thanks a lot for your program.
>
> **Judit Pauka**
> **Life Coach - Change Specialist**
> **www.jpevolutioncoaching.com**

> Since the very first secret I have been starting my day with a smile on my face. It's a beautiful way to start the day and has guaranteed that my day goes well. I have since passed the secret on to many people and they are also using it to start their day on a good note! Thanks so much Duane for the really practical, really easy to use tips!
>
> **Christie Pinto**
> **Personal Coaching, Workshops and Retreats**
> **Bali Awakening Guided Harmony Holidays**
> **www.crystalclearhorizons.biz**

> The morning I did my first of the 7 secrets, I smiled, stretched said Thank You, left the phones alone, looked out of the window and saw beautiful, glorious flowers and looked back inside to immediately glance in the mirror and see ME!!!!!! how funny is that... two beautiful things heehee.
>
> Keep being brilliant, you do it so well.
>
> Love, light and laughter
>
> **Karen x**

Thank you for your secrets. I love them and have already a smile stuck on my face and it's just day 1.

Love Light and Laughter

Marie

I do wake up and say thank you and find beauty inside and out. I was used to finding things outside myself, but now finding beauty inside is really cool! Having a positive outlook the moment I awake, sets my mindset for peace and happiness for the day. Truly magical.

The other big "ah-hah" for me was letting others do deeds for me! Being in a new relationship has allowed me to let them do things for me, where in the past I have always been the one doing everything. This doesn't allow my partner to feel good and I think men do like this!

Thanks Duane for sharing this program with all of us!

Love, Tania

I joined and completed the 7 Minute Secrets back in September. I enjoyed it immensely because it really made me focus on some of the specifics. It also helped me gain clarity and I am now truly unstoppable! I especially like waking every morning and smiling before I open my eyes; and then I feast my happy little soul on the pix next to my bed before moving out to my beautiful garden!

Thank you Duane... it's a piece of inspiration and everyone should do it!!!

Hugs,

Penelope Jane Whiteley

My story - Donna Powell

7 minutes a day... such a small amount of time really. When I first saw the secrets I wasn't really sure what to expect...

I mean what difference could 7 minutes a day make really?

Now, having used the secrets and morning ritual for several months, what I love is that no matter where I am, what I've been dreaming about or how I wake up - whether naturally or by the alarm clock sounding in my ear, those precious moments of smile, stretch and say thank you as my feet hit the floor always set me up for a great day. I do it automatically now, without even thinking. I loved the little bit of me time that practising the 7 minute secrets has given me each day.

It's a chance to focus on me and do a little check in every day of where I'm at with my life and goals I want to achieve. It's a great way to consciously make choices and take steps in the right direction for me.

Thank you Duane for showing me the impact of what you can achieve just by taking a little bit of time each day to stop, breathe, and assess.

For me, stopping to reward myself has been the biggest thing as previously this was something I wasn't good at - I was always focussed on doing it, and moving onto the next thing. Setting out and planning rewards for myself has made the whole process of achievement a lot more enjoyable, and made me realise that enjoying the journey along the way AND celebrating how far I've come (instead of focussing on what I haven't done) is much more fun and I'd rather live life that way and enjoy my successes.

Thank you for being such a special person and giving me this gift. Or rather teaching me how to give myself this gift.

Love Don xo

Donna Powell
London NW3 5NB
To call/txt from o'seas +44 7796 282 733

About the author: Duane Alley

Trainer | Author | Speaker | Coach

Duane Alley spent the first 15 years of his professional life working with some of the biggest and fastest growing retail and franchise businesses in the country; he then spent 5 years as Head Trainer & Coach for one of the biggest Personal Development companies on the planet.

He has combined his extensive experience from the business world in delivering real world results with his success and study of personal development, rapid human change and shifting consciousness.

As a Master Trainer, Author, Speaker and Performance Coach he now works with businesses and entrepreneurs quickly and easily improve their businesses and make more money and with individuals, couples and families to make simple changes and take small steps to live better lives day by day.

Keep in touch:

- www.duanealley.com
- www.facebook.com/duanealleypage
- www.twitter.com/DuaneAlley
- www.youtube.com/duanealley
- success@duanealley.com

Introduction

Foreword

Introduction:
Foreword

Congratulations on picking up this book and welcome!

It's your first step on the road to success! Very soon you'll be getting into my *7 Minute Secrets* which will help your business grow and bring success into your life from all angles.

You can read this book all at once or save a chapter per day. In any case, you'll want to do the book chapter by chapter daily even if you've read it through once.

This book is loaded with a little inspiration & action to charge you up. I will be providing you with a brand new approach to planning and living your week to get the most out of every moment and have you LOVING IT!

The only thing you need to do apart from reading this book is to commit 7 Minutes every morning this week to start something incredible — FOR YOU. Then, I've provided for you six weeks' worth of journal space for you to follow up for a month and a bit till you get the hang of the *7 Minute Secrets*.

You can use your own journal, but I highly recommend having a journal of some kind and a pen. There's only a little you will want to write down each day.

Also, you can check out my website for a wealth of information.

Go to: www.duanealley.com

If you have any questions at all, don't hesitate to email me directly, or hit the reply button to any of the messages. You can even snail mail me.

Also, if you have any topic ideas for our newsletter or an article idea, don't hesitate to send me a message.

While browsing and while reading your emails and this book, always remember my motto: "*Fun, Laughter and Green Lights.*"

Duane Alley
Creator/Author, The 7 Secrets Series
DuaneAlley Training and DuaneAlley Coaching

Day 0

BONUS
7 Minute Secret

Day 0:
BONUS *7 Minute Secret*

I start my book with a bonus!

It's funny, because most people wait till the end of something (or near the end) to throw out a bonus. I've never been one to wait for what I wanted and because I love getting bonuses I wanted to give you one straight up. There will even be more later too!

You know - this bonus is more than just "extra" strategies. That's partly why it comes right at the beginning of the book. Because it can really set the entire tone for what you will be doing and building on through the whole *7 Minute Secret* book.

The *7 Minute Secret* program is designed for you to be able to achieve each step, every day within around seven minutes. It's a secret (or can be), because people will start to wonder what "secret" you know that has you so energised, excited and "into" life now.

The truth is, that you'll want to "get into" your day and week with more enthusiasm and passion than maybe ever before. The absolute best time to work with the strategies I am going to share with you is in the morning, at the start of each day. You can do it right after waking up before hitting the shower, or during breakfast or on the way to work. But it's best to really set aside seven minutes solely to spend on these thoughts.

You can then use them as a springboard to launch yourself into the adventure that lies ahead. Even if it doesn't feel that way now — by next week you'll be feeling a little different about your days.

Now, without further ado, I'll move onto the bonus secret.

Secret Zero — the first Bonus. It's not when we wake up — the answer is HOW we wake up. And then what we do straight after. Try this tomorrow and then for every one of the next seven days as I reveal each of the *7 Minute Secrets* and you get to learn their power and effect on your life...

① **Wake up whenever you do.** When you know you are awake, maybe even before you open your eyes do ONE thing — SMILE! That's all... eyes closed and SMILE.

② **Keep smiling and STRETCH a little** — like a cat waking up from a nap.

③ **Keep smiling and while you do your little stretch** — **OUT LOUD say the words "THANK YOU!"** — quiet, loud, full voice or whispered — doesn't matter. All that matters is that you say it. People sometimes say, "For what?" — don't worry about it — you will fill in the blanks, at least unconsciously and that's what matters.

④ You'll notice at no time have I said — turn on your phone — that's because **I am going to challenge you to LEAVE THE PHONE OFF** for at least the first hour of being awake (it's a challenge for a reason — some will do it, some won't be able to — it's up to you; but if someone needs to get in touch with you they will call your house or hotel) — you deserve a little of what I call "unplugged time".

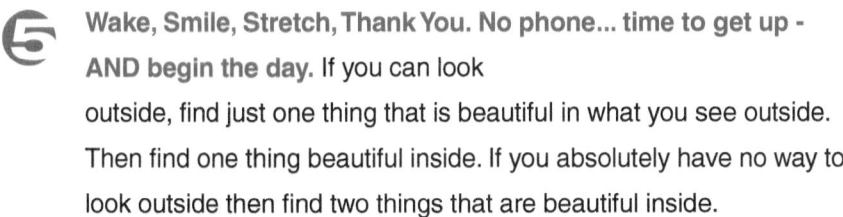 **Wake, Smile, Stretch, Thank You. No phone... time to get up - AND begin the day.** If you can look
outside, find just one thing that is beautiful in what you see outside. Then find one thing beautiful inside. If you absolutely have no way to look outside then find two things that are beautiful inside.

 You're up now so **have a nice drink of good room-temperature water.**

 **Time to begin your day and your *7 Minute Secret* for the day.**

In the next chapter you'll be getting your first *7 Minute Secret*. Do everything up to and including Step 6 and see what the day brings.

I hope your day is a magnificent day. Fill it with fun, laughter and green lights at every turn!

Today...

Fill out this daily report to help you keep track of your 7 minutes.

1 ...this made me smile today:

_____

2 ...I've stretched a little ◯ Yes ◯ No

3 ...I thanked life for:

_____

4 ...the phone was off from _____ to _____

5 ...I found beauty in:

_____
_____

6 ...I've drunk water: ▯ ▯ ▯ ▯ ▯ ▯ ▯ ▯

7 ...my *7 Minute Secret* for the day:

_____

Day 1
The Secret
of Rewarding Yourself

Day 1:
The Secret of Rewarding Yourself

The Program is designed for you to be able to achieve each step, every day in around 7 Minutes. People will start wondering why you are so energised, excited and "into" life now. This is why the steps can be "secret"! After taking these steps you'll want to "get into" your day and week with more enthusiasm and passion than ever before.

The morning is the absolute best time to work with the strategies I am going to share with you. The start of each day can then be used as a springboard to launch yourself into the adventure that lies ahead during the day, week and the rest of your life. At the start you may not feel much, but by next week you'll be feeling a little different about your days for sure.

Don't forget to take notes in your journal and write a few things down every day. Keep a pen by your bedside with your journal.

Just a quick recap of the Starting Secret of how your new day begins...

So what's the first of the **7 Minute Secrets** — it's easy.
Nod your head and say it with me..."easy".

In fact they all are — there are only 3 things you need to write down each day (they change each day).

WHAT YOU NEED TO KNOW:

> **Most people focus so intently on the achievement of a goal or goals.** What they forget or have never been taught is that the achievement of a goal is a fixed point in time. It is a single event that happens and once done is over. What we truly want to be focussed on is the creating of the life we want after we have achieved the goal. After all, the reason we achieved the goal was to have the life we get afterwards — make sense?

> **We get so hung up on "achievement"** as the ultimate aim that we forego the real reward which is living an incredible life as we design it or choose it to be.

> This is the reason that so many people I speak with in seminars and when I begin coaching them can give me a laundry list of past achievements and a litany of "what they're working on now".
> When, however, I ask them how they have rewarded themselves lately all I get are blank looks.

Today... Journal Day 1

Rewards create positive emotions and expansive feelings that drive us forward to greater achievements.

This is why you get to plan your rewards right now!

1) Grab your journal and pen

2) Write down 3 things you will do this week (in the next 7 days) to REWARD YOURSELF:

▶

▶

▶

3. Commit to them. Plan them. Do them.

Day 2
The Secret of Giving Green Lights

Day 2:
The Secret of Giving Green Lights

Welcome to Day 2!

The Program is designed for you to be able to achieve each step, every day within around 7 Minutes... and it's a secret (or can be) because people will start to wonder what "secret" you know that has you so energised, excited and "into" life now. The truth is you'll want to "Get into" your day and week with more enthusiasm and passion than ever before.

You will want your Journal to write just a few things down this morning... make sure you have that and a pen.

Remember — the Starting Secret — here's a quick overview reminder of how your new day begins...

Yesterday was easy... EASY. So is today!

In fact they all are - there are only 3 things you need to write down again (they change each day).

WHAT YOU NEED TO KNOW:

> **People are motivated for the most part more by what they can do for someone else** than by what they can do for themselves.

> **When it comes to human nature we can either fight it (not the best option most of the time) or work with it** to achieve an even greater result and create an even more magnificent life... maybe not surprisingly that's the one we're going with this morning.

> How many times have you heard of someone's struggles after the fact and thought, "I could have helped. I wish I'd known what you needed." Or something to that extent? If you are like most people in the world, probably more times than you wish to remember. Each of us is in a unique position to be us and we each have unique perspectives and skills. Sometimes it is so easy to do the most simple thing and yet it makes the biggest difference in another's life or work (or both). I call this GREEN-LIGHT GIVING.

> We do it not for the thanks; we do it for the fact that it really does feel good to know we have been able to help someone truly, sincerely and unselfishly just by doing what it is we can do.

Today... Journal Day 2

What you get to do now:

1) Grab your journal and pen

2) Write down 3 things you will do this week (in the next 7 Days) to GIVE THE GREENLIGHT TO ANOTHER (it can be for one or different people)

▶ _____

▶ _____

▶ _____

3) Commit — Plan — Do

Third *7 Minute Secret* comes tomorrow so re-read this and Get Into It!

Have a magnificent day. Fill it with fun, laughter and green lights at every turn!

Duane

Day 3

The Secret of Asking for Green Lights

Day 3:
The Secret of Asking for Green Lights

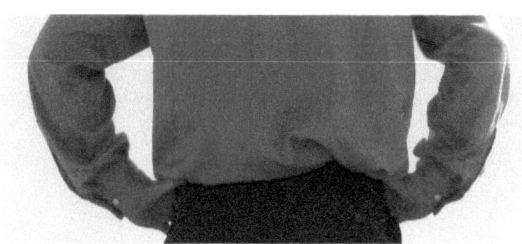

Welcome to Day 3!

By now you might be getting into the swing of things with the *7 Minute Secret Strategies.* Remember to keep your Journal handy with a pen.

And please remember — the Starting Secret — here's a quick overview reminder of how your new day begins...

40

WHAT YOU NEED TO KNOW:

Yesterday I wrote that, "people are motivated for the most part more by what they can do for someone else than by what they can do for themselves".

> **This is absolutely true** and as you imagine now what it is going to be like for you to have cleared 3 paths for others this week... How good do you feel? Even without their thanks (which I'm sure you will get plenty of) it feels great to genuinely help another do what it is they want to do or get what it is they want to get.

> **We all know how good it also feels to give a gift, right?** So it's time to give the gift of "Greenlighting" to another. I call this Greenlight Allowance.

You are going to let someone else help you. I want to be really honest here — this one will require you to "put yourself out there" beyond your "normal zone" (for most of us anyway). You want others to feel good about helping you too, so you'll be asking them for a green light to do something.

You can even ask the same people who you helped. This is the principle of "You scratch my back I'll scratch yours."

Today... Journal Day 3

What you get to do now:

1) Grab your journal and pen

2) Write down 3 things you can allow others (in the next 7 Days) to GIVE YOU SOME GREEN LIGHTS ON (if can be for one or different people)

- ▸ _____

- ▸ _____

- ▸ _____

3) Where's the push — here! You will need to ASK other people to help you!

Believe me, the temporary discomfort of asking others is washed away by the gratitude they will truly feel for you ALLOWING them to do so — watch and see

4) Commit — Plan — Do

Fourth *7 Minute Secret* comes tomorrow so re-read this and Get Into It!
Have a magnificent day. Fill it with fun, laughter and green lights at every turn!

Day 4
The Secret of Gratitude

Day 4:
The Secret of Gratitude

Welcome to Day 4!

So far you have learned four simple and powerful strategies that can begin to reshape what you are looking for on a daily and weekly basis. Today is no different...

Please remember — the Starting Secret — here's a quick overview reminder of how your new day begins...

WHAT YOU NEED TO KNOW:

> **Living with the attitude of gratitude** has been talked, written, sung, shouted and sold forever. There are CD sets, Seminars, Webinars, books and journals galore all preaching the same thing. Why? Because it is TRUE.

> **Living in the knowledge and state of gratitude** brings a sense of peace, abundance and grace to our lives that quite simply attracts more of the same.

Many times though, I hear people attempting to list everything they could possibly be grateful for in one list or just listing off the same ones over and over again. This type of treatment becomes a chore or a bore anyway you look at it.

Just because you thought it last week and didn't say it today doesn't mean you are not grateful for it... you are simply finding more and more in life to hold that place and state of grace, abundance and gratitude for in your mind, heart and life.

So when you get into today's *7 Minute Secret* I want you to think of some new things you can list... It's worth it... and it doesn't mean you are not grateful for everything else - just that you are finding EVEN MORE.

Today... Journal Day 4

What you get to do now:

1) Grab your journal and pen

2) Write down 3 things you are GRATEFUL FOR in your life

- ▸
- ▸
- ▸

3) W A R N I N G —You may be smiling a lot today!

Fifth *7 Minute Secret* comes tomorrow so re-read this and Get Into It!
Have a magnificent day. Fill it with fun, laughter and green lights at every turn!

Duane

Day 5

The Secret
of Gratitude
to Others

Day 5:
The Secret of Gratitude to Others

Welcome to Day 5!

"Wow, Duane, it seems like only a little while ago we began this trip together... and we've covered some great ground together so far."

By now, I imagine you would have started to reap the benefits of your 7 Minutes you've been secreting away every morning. Maybe you've rewarded yourself a couple of times by now; created some Green Lights for some friends, family or colleagues; even maybe asked for a Green Light to help yourself; and certainly you have three incredible new things to remember you are grateful for.

If any of this isn't happening then you get to remember today, right now... that nothing worth having can be gotten without DOING. What does that mean? Once you write your three things every morning - you've got to plan to do them and then GET INTO IT! Go do it...

Keep me and others informed too - let us share in your success... send me a message to let me know how you are going or even better post a message on the wall of my Official Site and inspire others by your success.

Time to get into today...

Please remember — the Starting Secret — here's a quick overview reminder of how your new day begins...

WHAT YOU NEED TO KNOW:

On the very first morning (well second really) of Day 1, I wrote about how people are so very caught up in achievement that they often times forget to focus on what they are creating along the way and afterwards.

In your new morning wake up routine (Step 3) is to say Thank You. We're going to bring those two ideas together today.

> **Feeling gratitude for what we have and where we are helps** create a state of abundance and grace in us — we know this and have experienced it.

> **What if you could bring that as a gift to others?**

That's what today's *7 Minute Secret* is about... not just saying "Thank you" to the universe but actually finding and thanking a specific person in your life.

Today... Journal Day 5

What you get to do now:

1) Grab your journal and pen

2) Write down 3 people you want to THANK for whatever reason. Write down who you want to thank and for what reason & WHEN you will do it

👤 WHO:	👤 WHO:	👤 WHO:
? WHY:	? WHY:	? WHY:
📅 WHEN:	📅 WHEN:	📅 WHEN:

3) Commit — Plan — Do

Sixth *7 Minute Secret* comes tomorrow so re-read this and Get Into It!
Have a magnificent day. Fill it with fun, laughter and green lights at every turn!

Duane

Day 6
The Secret of Doing

Day 6:
The Secret of Doing

Welcome to Day 6!

I imagine that many of your early *7 Minute Secret* tasks are being completed. I want you to get excited about the different elements of your life that you have touched on in the last few days.

> How good do you feel knowing you are rewarding yourself and helping others?

> What positive impact is it having on your life and work that you are free to ask for help and Green Lights not to mention the flow on effect when others realise by your example it is okay to ask?

> Think back to those 3 Things you are Grateful for and I wonder if your mind is flooded with even more gratitude?

You may not have made the time yet to thank someone (or you may — either way) you know the impact that will have. Don't you?

It is remarkable what you can do in and with just 7 Minutes each day, huh?

Time to get into today...

Please remember — the Starting Secret — here's a quick overview reminder of how your new day begins...

WHAT YOU NEED TO KNOW:

Today is a little different. There are still 3 Things to occupy your *7 Minutes*. You'll still be writing things down and there will be actions to take.

I mentioned previously that "there is nothing worth having or getting that you don't have have to work for" — in short — you can't have without doing!

So today I want you to think in a different way about what truly needs to be done this week (over the next 7 days).

Doing can ONLY stall at one of 3 places though:

> Starting

> Stopping

> Carrying on

That's it — nothing really fancy or complicated here and yet most of us have many things needing DOING that are stalled at one of these places. In fact we probably all stalled in each of these places with at least one piece of un-started, un-finished or un-moving action. It's time to find the gold, bank the gold or dig it up... I call this secret 3 Pieces of Gold.

Time to Get Into It!

Today... Journal Day 6

What you get to do now:

1) Grab your journal and pen

2) Write down 3 Things you Get to Take Action on this week that will bring great results to you

- _____
- _____
- _____

3) Write down 1 Thing that you need to START and what you are going to do this week to start (and when)

I will Start...

_____

What I will do to start...

_____

4) Write down 1 Thing that you need to FINISH and what you are going to do this week to finish the job/task (and when)

I will Start...

What I will do to start...

5) Write down 1 Thing that you need to KEEP MOVING ON and what you are going to do this week to move the project/task forward (and when)

I need...

To move forward...

6) Commit — Do — Get into it!

My last *7 Minute Secret* comes tomorrow so re-read this and Get Into It!
Have a magnificent day. Fill it with fun, laughter and green lights at every turn!

Duane

Day 7

Your Last 7 Minute
Secret...
Sort Of...

Day 7:
Your Last 7 Minute Secret... Sort Of...

Welcome to Day 7!

It's been a fun few days - with lots of seeds planted along the way — I can imagine many of those seeds have sprouted and new ways of looking at the world are taking root.

I have seen this in myself when I put together these secrets from a number of different sources and ideas — some from incredible masters, some of my own and some just common sense. And we are almost at the end of this sharing time. If you haven't already, make sure you have signed up for my Newsletter so that I can keep you updated with new developments and future sharings.

For now though, it's time to get into today...

Please remember — the Starting Secret — here's a quick overview reminder of how your new day begins...

WHAT YOU NEED TO KNOW:

There has been much good come from the last week and just as a farmer uses the remnants of the last harvest as the nutrients for the next... we will look back soon on all the greatness you have created in order to stimulate and excite you for what is to come.

I adapted this final *7 Minute Secret* from my own Annual Goal Setting Process. By identifying some of the best moments and excitements of the week before we not only reward ourselves by appreciating what we have accomplished we also condition our minds to accept the possibility (and soon enough) probability of even greater success next week.

Today... Journal Day 7

What you get to do now:

1) Grab your journal and pen

2) Write down 3 Things you feel GREAT or Most Proud of from last week's achievements

- _____
- _____
- _____

3. Commit — Plan — Do

Our Seven 7 Minute Secrets have been shared and learnt... BUT... There's another BONUS tomorrow — I'll see you then.

Till then, as always... Have a magnificent day. Fill it with fun, laughter and green lights at every turn!

Duane

Conclusion
Afterthoughts

Conclusion: Afterthoughts

You made it all the way to the end of the *7 Minute Secret* Program and have already started to see a lot of great things and different focus occurring in your life and planning. No doubt, because we staggered the days, you have so much more to come over the next few days as well...

WHAT YOU NEED TO KNOW:

> **The *7 Minute Secret Program* was designed to build each Strategy upon the last and create a snowball effect** of change in the way you view or plan for your week ahead. Simply by getting to write down those 3 things every morning you were shifting your focus for the next 7 Days from what you HAD to do or whatever came along to what you GET to do — a far more powerful approach and thought process.
>
> Imagine now if every one of your weeks began that way... with your focus shifted to the excitement, adventure, fun and gratitude for a brilliant week ahead.
>
> Think of how you would be looking back on all the magnificent days and the life you would be creating at an even greater level...

That's what the *7 Minute Secret Program* was all about. Building into you a system for designing a week of wonder from the get go.

That's why I've included six weeks' worth (that's six times seven!) of journal pages for you to continue doing these seven steps for just over a month to make it become part of your daily routine for the rest of your life.

This is your mission — if you choose to accept it.

6 weeks
Workbook

Week 1

What you get to do now:

1) Grab your journal and pen

2) Write down 3 Things you will do this week to reward yourself (big things or simple things — doesn't matter)

▸

▸

▸

3. Write down 3 Things you will do this to give a Green Light to another

▸

▸

▸

4) Write down 3 Things you can ask others to do (and allow them to) to give you Green Lights

▸

▸

▸

5 Write down 3 Things you are grateful for in your life (make them different)

▶

▶

▶

6 Write down 3 People you will thank this week (& reason)

▶

▶

▶

7 Write down 3 Things you get to take action on this week that will being greater results to you (1 x Start, 1 x Finish, 1 x Keep Moving)

▶

▶

▶

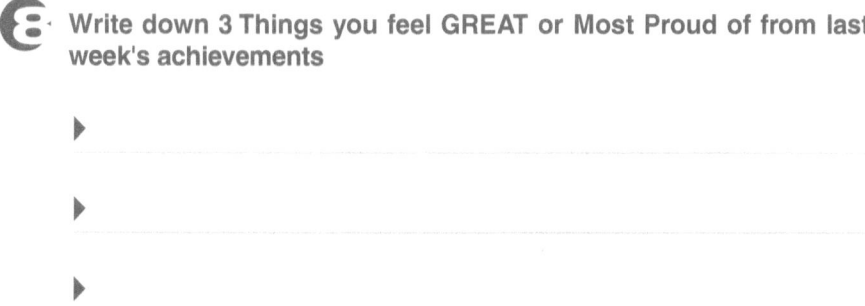 Write down 3 Things you feel GREAT or Most Proud of from last week's achievements

▶

▶

▶

For those things that can be planned into your week ahead — go ahead and plan them out. Make sure you allocate dates and times where possible. Remember: Commit — Plan — Get Into It! The great news is that now you are familiar with the strategy and new way of thinking they become easier to think of and faster to write down and plan.

Of course every day begins with the New Way of Waking that you have been practising all week:

Week 2

What you get to do now:

1) Grab your journal and pen

2) Write down 3 Things you will do this week to reward yourself (big things or simple things — doesn't matter)

▶

▶

▶

3. Write down 3 Things you will do this to give a Green Light to another

▶

▶

▶

4) Write down 3 Things you can ask others to do (and allow them to) to give you Green Lights

▶

▶

▶

5. Write down 3 Things you are grateful for in your life (make them different)

▸

▸

▸

6. Write down 3 People you will thank this week (& reason)

▸

▸

▸

7. Write down 3 Things you get to take action on this week that will being greater results to you (1 x Start, 1 x Finish, 1 x Keep Moving)

▸

▸

▸

8. Write down 3 Things you feel GREAT or Most Proud of from last week's achievements

▶ _____

▶ _____

▶ _____

For those things that can be planned into your week ahead — go ahead and plan them out. Make sure you allocate dates and times where possible. Remember: Commit — Plan — Get Into It! The great news is that now you are familiar with the strategy and new way of thinking they become easier to think of and faster to write down and plan.

Of course every day begins with the New Way of Waking that you have been practising all week:

Week 3

What you get to do now:

1) Grab your journal and pen

2) Write down 3 Things you will do this week to reward yourself (big things or simple things — doesn't matter)

▸

▸

▸

3) Write down 3 Things you will do this to give a Green Light to another

▸

▸

▸

4) Write down 3 Things you can ask others to do (and allow them to) to give you Green Lights

▸

▸

▸

5 Write down 3 Things you are grateful for in your life (make them different)

▶ _____

▶ _____

▶ _____

6 Write down 3 People you will thank this week (& reason)

▶ _____

▶ _____

▶ _____

7 Write down 3 Things you get to take action on this week that will being greater results to you (1 x Start, 1 x Finish, 1 x Keep Moving)

▶ _____

▶ _____

▶ _____

8. Write down 3 Things you feel GREAT or Most Proud of from last week's achievements

▶

▶

▶

For those things that can be planned into your week ahead — go ahead and plan them out. Make sure you allocate dates and times where possible. Remember: Commit — Plan — Get Into It! The great news is that now you are familiar with the strategy and new way of thinking they become easier to think of and faster to write down and plan.

Of course every day begins with the New Way of Waking that you have been practising all week:

Week 4

What you get to do now:

1) Grab your journal and pen

2) Write down 3 Things you will do this week to reward yourself (big things or simple things — doesn't matter)

▶
▶
▶

3. Write down 3 Things you will do this to give a Green Light to another

▶
▶
▶

4) Write down 3 Things you can ask others to do (and allow them to) to give you Green Lights

▶
▶
▶

5. Write down 3 Things you are grateful for in your life (make them different)

▸

▸

▸

6. Write down 3 People you will thank this week (& reason)

▸

▸

▸

7. Write down 3 Things you get to take action on this week that will being greater results to you (1 x Start, 1 x Finish, 1 x Keep Moving)

▸

▸

▸

3. Write down 3 Things you feel GREAT or Most Proud of from last week's achievements

▸

▸

▸

For those things that can be planned into your week ahead — go ahead and plan them out. Make sure you allocate dates and times where possible. Remember: Commit — Plan — Get Into It! The great news is that now you are familiar with the strategy and new way of thinking they become easier to think of and faster to write down and plan.

Of course every day begins with the New Way of Waking that you have been practising all week:

Week 5

What you get to do now:

1) Grab your journal and pen

2) Write down 3 Things you will do this week to reward yourself (big things or simple things — doesn't matter)

▶ _____

▶ _____

▶ _____

3. Write down 3 Things you will do this to give a Green Light to another

▶ _____

▶ _____

▶ _____

4) Write down 3 Things you can ask others to do (and allow them to) to give you Green Lights

▶ _____

▶ _____

▶ _____

5. Write down 3 Things you are grateful for in your life (make them different)

▶ _____

▶ _____

▶ _____

6. Write down 3 People you will thank this week (& reason)

▶ _____

▶ _____

▶ _____

7. Write down 3 Things you get to take action on this week that will being greater results to you (1 x Start, 1 x Finish, 1 x Keep Moving)

▶ _____

▶ _____

▶ _____

8. **Write down 3 Things you feel GREAT or Most Proud of from last week's achievements**

▶ _____

▶ _____

▶ _____

For those things that can be planned into your week ahead — go ahead and plan them out. Make sure you allocate dates and times where possible. Remember: Commit — Plan — Get Into It! The great news is that now you are familiar with the strategy and new way of thinking they become easier to think of and faster to write down and plan.

Of course every day begins with the New Way of Waking that you have been practising all week:

Week 6

What you get to do now:

1) Grab your journal and pen

2) Write down 3 Things you will do this week to reward yourself (big things or simple things — doesn't matter)

▸

▸

▸

3. Write down 3 Things you will do this to give a Green Light to another

▸

▸

▸

4) Write down 3 Things you can ask others to do (and allow them to) to give you Green Lights

▸

▸

▸

5. Write down 3 Things you are grateful for in your life (make them different)

-
-
-

6. Write down 3 People you will thank this week (& reason)

-
-
-

7. Write down 3 Things you get to take action on this week that will being greater results to you (1 x Start, 1 x Finish, 1 x Keep Moving)

-
-
-

8. **Write down 3 Things you feel GREAT or Most Proud of from last week's achievements**

▶ _____

▶ _____

▶ _____

For those things that can be planned into your week ahead — go ahead and plan them out. Make sure you allocate dates and times where possible. Remember: Commit — Plan — Get Into It! The great news is that now you are familiar with the strategy and new way of thinking they become easier to think of and faster to write down and plan.

Of course every day begins with the New Way of Waking that you have been practising all week:

Week 7

What you get to do now:

1 Grab your journal and pen

2 Write down 3 Things you will do this week to reward yourself (big things or simple things — doesn't matter)

▶

▶

▶

3 Write down 3 Things you will do this to give a Green Light to another

▶

▶

▶

4 Write down 3 Things you can ask others to do (and allow them to) to give you Green Lights

▶

▶

▶

5 Write down 3 Things you are grateful for in your life (make them different)

▶
▶
▶

6 Write down 3 People you will thank this week (& reason)

▶
▶
▶

7 Write down 3 Things you get to take action on this week that will being greater results to you (1 x Start, 1 x Finish, 1 x Keep Moving)

▶
▶
▶

8. Write down 3 Things you feel GREAT or Most Proud of from last week's achievements

▶

▶

▶

For those things that can be planned into your week ahead — go ahead and plan them out. Make sure you allocate dates and times where possible. Remember: Commit — Plan — Get Into It! The great news is that now you are familiar with the strategy and new way of thinking they become easier to think of and faster to write down and plan.

Of course every day begins with the New Way of Waking that you have been practising all week:

Keep me and others informed too — let everyone share in your success and joy. Send me a message to let me know how you are going or even better post a message on the wall of my **Official Page on Facebook** (www.facebook.com/duanealleypage) and inspire others by your success.

Till then, as always...

Have a magnificent day.

Fill it with fun, laughter and green lights all the way,

Duane

NOTES

NOTES

www.ingramcontent.com/pod-product-compliance
Lightning Source LLC
Chambersburg PA
CBHW022019290426
44109CB00015B/1238